Awesome Supervisory Skills:
Seven Lessons for Young, First-Time Managers

Written by Tamara Murray
Edited by Eva C. Meszaros

*To the people who've mentored me, I learned all of this
by watching you—thank you.*

*To the awesome young leaders who feel like imposters,
you are, in reality, the best people for the job.*

Contents

Welcome to Your First Day of Awesome Management   9

Lesson 1: Management Is a Service Job   11
Lesson 2: "Um, What Did I Do Today?" Is Normal   15
Lesson 3: Make 'Em Long for the Sea   19
Lesson 4: Deal With Bad Apples Faster Than
         You Can Read This Sentence   23
Lesson 5: You Have a Team for a Reason   27
Lesson 6: Would You Respect You?   31
Lesson 7: Secure Your Mask First   35

Pay It Forward   39

Resources and Recommended Reading   41
About the Author   43

Welcome to Your First Day of Awesome Management

Congratulations, you've been promoted to manager! At the tender age of however-old-you-are!

You texted your significant other with a minimum of 15 exclamation marks. You called your mom to tell her you've made it, you've finally made it. And you treated yourself to an adult beverage, or three, in anticipation of your raise.

Then, you bought this guide. Being the smarty pants you are, you know that the number one reason people hate their jobs is because their boss sucks. And you don't want to suck as a manager—you want to be *awesome*. But how?

That's how it is for most people: once you're really good at something, you stop doing it and start managing other people to do it. But what made you awesome at your initial job isn't necessarily what will make you an awesome manager. And it can be especially challenging when you're one of the youngest in the room and without formal management training.

A wise manager of mine once told me that you learn the most when you're in over your head. In this book, you'll gain the biggest lessons I've learned during my time as a young manager—in over my head. You'll also find real-world examples of how to apply these lessons immediately.

I found my footing through a combination of trial and error, reading a lot of *Fast Company*, and having the occasional breakdown in a colleague's office. Eventually, I had people telling me I was the best manager they'd ever had.

You're already on track to being an awesome manager because you are humble enough to admit you could use some advice. Everyone brings their own style and ideas as they find their footing as a manager. Hopefully these lessons will help you fast-forward through some of the growing pains and be the awesome, confident, capable manager you know you can be.

Lesson 1:
Management Is a Service Job

In 2007, I was at a dinner discussion to hear advice from women further in their careers. The food was forgettable and I was distracted thinking about the hour and two forms of public transit it would take to get home.

But then, our guest speaker said something that surprised me: "Being a manager is about removing barriers for other people."

I wrote it down, even though I didn't fully understand what it meant until years later.

There are many people I've managed who were smarter than me. I'm quick on the uptake, but sometimes someone had more years on me. Sometimes we had the same experience, but they would see patterns I couldn't, come up with ideas I didn't. It scared me.

One guy I managed was like an encyclopedia of U.S. history and politics, and could probably hold his own in a public policy debate against five Harvard professors. Another woman I managed could comb through vast amounts of complex data—demographic information, web analytics, health trends. Not only could she understand it, but she could make the information *exciting* to other people.

Often I found myself asking, *how can I be an awesome manager if I'm not the smartest person in the room?*

As it turns out, even really smart people need help sometimes. One of my direct reports stopped by my office one morning with a big problem: in just two hours, she and another manager were set to give an important presentation—and the manager had just called in with a medical emergency.

Our client would not be happy. The presentation was already postponed once, and this additional delay would set the whole project back and worsen an already tense relationship.

We started listing our options. I couldn't call the client because she didn't know me from a hole in the ground. Telling the other manager to suck it up and come in wasn't a possibility since she was being prepped for surgery. My direct report could do the presentation solo, but there were some pieces only her co-presenter knew. Plus, the client wants and pays for both of their time.

In the end, there was only one realistic option: my direct report had to call the client to postpone. Not an impossible task, but a very delicate one.

I advised her to lay out the other options for the client, along with the recommendation to postpone, so the client felt like she had some say in the matter. She was nervous about delivering such bad news to an already frustrated client, so we did a role play so I could give her pointers and boost her confidence. Then, off my colleague went to make the call.

Not only did the client understand the situation, but she appreciated the opportunity to weigh in on the decision. The two of them even went on to discuss ways to keep the project timeline on track despite the delay. And the working relationship improved because of the transparency.

* * *

Your job as a manager is to, first, provide clear context about the work (we'll talk about this more later) and, second, remove any roadblocks in your employee's way. Maybe they need advice on how to deal with a difficult situation, more information about the task, help getting started, permission to spend less time on another project, more budget, cooperation from other departments, and so on.

It's *not* your job to be the smartest person in the room. Being a manager is about serving your team—helping them succeed at their work—not being "the boss." It's one of the biggest rules first-time managers don't get.

Even if you are the smartest person in the room, your team is made up of smart people, too. They want to be engaged and challenged by their work. When presented with a task, they'll figure out how to make it happen and ask for help when they need it. In fact, research shows people are more likely to be happy and apply themselves if they have this kind of freedom at work. Don't you feel this way?

In other words, management is a service job. The service you provide, as the woman at the dinner discussion said, is removing barriers for your people.

When you shift your thinking of the job in this way, it creates a dynamic that everyone can respect, both folks at the entry-level and more seasoned co-workers. And it actually helps everyone get better work done.

Put Awesome Into Action

When talking with your team, use language that reinforces that you're there to help. Say out loud, "My job is to make sure you have what you need to do yours. If you're ever stuck, tell me and we'll figure it out." If something is going poorly, ask questions like, "What do we need to get this to look like *[describe the ideal]*?" Listen to your team's suggestions. If it's a problem they can't solve alone, that is now the biggest item on your to-do list.

Always follow through; you want your people to trust you. If you say you're going to help fix a problem, do it. But don't fret: if it's a roadblock you can't remove, that's OK as long as you did your best. Explain exactly what you did to try to fix it and be open to other ideas. It's important they know you exhausted your options.

Be proactive and don't wait for problems to arise. Even if everything is going well, make it a habit to check in with your team. Ask things like, "How are you doing? Is this challenging you? Do you have ideas we should try next time?"

Screamers never prosper. How are you supposed to remove barriers if your people are too afraid to talk to you? If someone makes a mistake, say, "Thank you for telling me. Let's figure out how to fix it. Also, what should we do differently next time to avoid this?" It reflects better on you when you're a problem-solver, and next time your people will come to you before a mistake is made.

Lesson 2:
"Um, What Did I Do Today?" Is Normal

Not long after becoming a manager at a PR firm, I walked into the director's office with an embarrassing admission.

"I ... I don't know what I did today," I said. "I know I went to a bunch of meetings, sent emails, and made phone calls. But I don't know what I *accomplished*."

He's a nice guy—and an awesome manager—so he smiled and told me to sit down so we could talk about it.

Most of us, early in our careers, are all about our to-do list. No matter what industry we're in, we're doing concrete, tangible stuff: conducting some research, ordering supplies, writing an article. At the end of the day, we look at our to-do list and reflect on how much we got done.

But as a manager, you don't *do* so much anymore. Other people do things, and you manage them. It's an important job, but it's harder to know whether your day was a win or a loss.

I met the head of a city government department in San Francisco who said there are days when she crosses absolutely nothing off her to-do list. She spends her days with the people in her department helping them. Maybe she's in her office on the phone, maybe she's having coffee with someone on her team.

She told me that was time well spent, even though it was sometimes exasperating to have a to-do list that grows rather than shrinks. She clearly understands that management is a service job. And my director said pretty much the same thing in response to my admission: how you judge your success as a manager is different from when you were a doer. Then, he wrote down three questions for me to ask myself at the end of every day.

Did I move things forward?
Remember, other people are doing the doing. Did you help them keep the work moving forward? Is everything on track?

Did I do the right things?
Maybe you only got one thing done, but it happened to be the biggest roadblock for your team. That's a win.

Did I delegate, and did I delegate well?
Don't spend time doing things others are perfectly capable of doing. Focus on doing the things only you can do. We'll talk about this more in subsequent lessons.

* * *

I wrote the questions down and put them on my wall, and then stopped feeling guilty about my to-do list. In fact, it brought back some earlier lessons from my first management role at a small retail store.

I was the assistant manager, but most days I didn't work with the people I managed or the people who managed me. No one did outside of peak, weekend hours.

One of the things the owner, who was pretty awesome herself, often did was leave a letter for the manager coming in the next day. The letter would include things like important shipments to watch for, custom orders to prioritize because they were approaching their due date, or updates on what already got done so there was no duplication. It was a simple but great little system.

But it also took time to create—sometimes over an hour—and not just because the lack of a computer meant the letters were handwritten. It was a mental exercise that took thoughtful direction and prioritization. What did tomorrow's employee need to focus on? What information or context did s/he need to get it right? What did I do today that they needed to be aware of?

Turns out, I had already learned the three questions my director shared with me. But what I still hadn't learned was that it was OK to spend my time that way: prioritizing, delegating, and spending time with those I managed. I thought that was icing on the cake of my to-do list. But actually, it was the heart of my job.

It takes time to manage. Spend the time gladly because, if you don't, no one else will.

Meet the Zorro Circle, Your New Best Friend

There's a scene in the movie *The Mask of Zorro* where Don Diego de la Vega (Anthony Hopkins) is training Alejandro Murrieta (Antonio Banderas) to become the next Zorro. But Murrieta is too blinded by his thirst for revenge, and overall drunkenness, to focus on his sword training.

De la Vega draws a circle with his sword in the dirt and tells Murrietta that, while training, nothing exists outside of that circle. The circle is his world; there is nothing else. Once he masters his swordsmanship in that circle, it can slowly expand.

Workplace happiness expert Shawn Achor talks about how this concept helps people at work too. Because your to-do list will always grow faster than it shrinks, it's easy to get distracted by the enormity of it all and accomplish nothing.

Draw your own Zorro Circle on a piece of paper. Pick the most important thing you can do for your team or project and put it in inside. Nothing else exists in your world until it's complete. No one will care about what you did or didn't do on your to-do list if you manage to fix the biggest problem your team is facing.

Put Awesome Into Action

Write down the three questions above and put them where you'll see them every day. Use them as a guide to establish your priorities at the beginning of the day, and make a habit of checking in with yourself at the end of the day to see how you did. You may not be able to answer "yes" to every question at first, but you'll get there.

Be religious about using Zorro Circles. Make one first thing in the morning with the most important barrier you can remove for your team today and stick to it. Once you're done, make another one, and so on. And who knows? Maybe the biggest problem one of your people is facing is needing his or her own Zorro Circle.

Carve out time to think. Leave the office, block out time on your calendar—whatever works for you. As a manager, you need to spend time thinking about how best to move the work forward, how to solve your team's roadblocks, and what to delegate to others. Don't think this is idle time; this is what you're paid to do.

Lesson 3:
Make 'Em Long for the Sea

"We'd like you to manage this account. It's really important and has the potential to grow into more business," I heard my manager say as I took notes on the whiteboard. I looked over my shoulder and realized he was talking to me.

"Hah! Nothing like a little pressure," I joked casually. My internal reaction? *Oh, crap.*

The goal was securing media coverage in 17 states with little time and not-so-new research about juvenile incarceration. My team was already overworked, and I was worried they'd write off the project as impossible.

Soon came the meeting to kick off the project and I watched my team quietly settling in around the table. A thought flashed through my mind: *what's going to motivate this group to pull this off?*

Following my gut, I jumped up and scribbled "ERMAD MEAT" on the wall. With as much energy as I could muster, I called out, "Quick! Who can unscramble this first?"

Everyone started chuckling until someone shouted, "Dream team!" Energy, momentum, and team spirit—that was my strategy. I laid out the project goals, the roles, and why, with this dream team, it was all doable.

But as we talked more about what was expected, you could see a dark cloud forming. It followed everyone back to their desks. Team spirit was important, but it wasn't enough.

I was debating whether the meeting was a win, loss, or draw when an email popped up. Someone on my team sent everyone a photo slideshow of teens—they were just kids, really—locked up in rundown jail cells. They looked so young.

Suddenly, emails began firing. They're locked up in state prisons with adults, one said. What happens to them when they get out?

And just like that, we found what mattered more than team spirit. Kids were being sent to adult prisons for petty crimes and losing any chance of a normal future. And the public needed to know.

* * *

There's a bakery in San Francisco called Craftsman and Wolves that my husband and I used to pop by when we felt like treating ourselves on Sunday mornings. They make a mean savory muffin called The Rebel Within that has a soft-boiled egg baked inside.

Once, while we were relishing every bite of muffin perfection, I looked up at the quotes on the bakery's walls. One stood out in particular, by Antoine de Saint-Exupéry.

"If you want to build a ship, don't drum up people to collect wood and don't assign them tasks and work, but rather teach them to long for the endless immensity of the sea."

Between that quote and the muffin, my mind was totally blown. A sub-lesson here is that wisdom can come from unexpected places.

Awesome managers rally their people around a common purpose that is bigger than themselves, or any individual task. They make their team want it so bad they can taste it. Because then, they're not working on a spreadsheet—they're improving health care. They're not rewriting code—they're making it possible for people across the world to work together. They're not making sales calls—they're making young people's college dreams come true.

That last one is a real example, by the way. In a 2007 experiment, Adam Grant of the University of Pennsylvania Wharton School found that call-center workers fundraising for a university's scholarship program were able to more than double their solicited donations after spending just *five minutes* hearing from a student who benefited from a scholarship.

As for my team's project, it was hard work. We blew through our budget and had to ask for more money. Reporters weren't returning our calls or emails. We had a necessary but painful two-hour conference call dedicated to getting facts straight.

But their longing for the sea was stronger. They ultimately got media coverage in 13 of 17 states, shining a light on the kids forgotten behind prison walls.

Make it about the goal, not the task. Your team will be motivated to get results, and you will too.

Put Awesome Into Action

Get to know your team. What motivates them? Is it competition, social good, big breakthroughs, or all of the above? Introduce the work that way, and make sure to remind people what it is they're really working for every chance you get. Get creative: send a daily email, put a physical object that represents the goal in the workspace, make special desktop wallpaper. Whatever keeps their eyes on the prize.

Bring people closer to what motivates them. The call-center workers got to meet a scholarship recipient. Go on a site visit or meet real customers or end-users. It's easier to get excited about people and places than a project timeline.

Help each individual understand why their role and tasks are important. For example, "Your job is to make sure the content on this website is always accurate and up-to-date. We can't create a tool that helps people get out of debt if we're giving them bad information." This one can be tough, especially if you're dealing with bright employees and an uninteresting project. It takes practice to show the right blend of enthusiasm and honesty.

Leave room for creativity. Now that you've gotten them to long for the sea, don't stifle your team by micromanaging how they build their ship. Give them necessary parameters—budget, deadline, safety requirements—and then let them run with it.

Lesson 4:
Deal With Bad Apples Faster Than
You Can Read This Sentence

"No one respects our expertise," my colleague grumbled during a planning meeting. "We'll come up with good ideas, but they'll just do what they want in the end—it's a waste of time."

Yikes. We've all felt this way at work before, myself included. But when he said this in front of the whole team, a silent alarm went off in my head.

Do not underestimate the influence of his statement. Will Felps of the Rotterdam School of Management conducted a study placing an actor playing one of three "bad apple" roles—jerk, slacker, or depressed pessimist—into workgroups. In every role and in every trial, the groups *without* the actor did better work. And in the groups *with* the actor, other people in the group started to mimic the actor's bad behavior.

In other words, a bad apple can spoil the bunch—and fast.

Another colleague spoke up: "I don't think it's a good use of our time either, especially if their minds are already made up." I saw the negative body language around the table and scrambled to redirect the conversation, but even my attitude was suffering.

"Look, whoever moves the fastest here will control the process and the outcome," I said in a sharp tone. "Let's just move fast and they won't have time to go against our recommendations." An accurate statement, but the tone was flippant and harsh. See how contagious attitudes are?

This is difficult to deal with as a manager. Especially if you agree with your colleagues—and I did in this case. But awesome managers understand they have different responsibilities: moving the work forward, removing barriers, and getting everyone focused on solutions. Ultimately I was able to do this, but only with help from my own manager.

* * *

I've managed all three of the bad apples from the experiment: jerks, slackers, and depressed pessimists. They put you in a tough position because if you spend too much time and energy on them, your rock stars notice. Why do a great job when your manager doesn't notice because s/he's too busy with the bad apple?

That's the opposite feeling you want to create, because you want your best people happy in their jobs. But if you completely ignore the bad apple, everyone's work suffers. So you have to nip the problem in the bud.

There are two solutions for bad apple behavior. First, talk to your bad apple about what you expect from them. Because your job is to serve your people, find out what barriers might be in their way and make a good-faith effort to fix them. I've had employees struggle because of frustrating projects, rude colleagues, and good ideas that went unnoticed. Even great employees go through tough times, so uncovering the root of the problem should do the trick.

Second, identify your rock star(s)—the motivated ones doing a good job—and reward their behavior publicly. You want to reinforce your message about what is expected, and one of the ways to do so is by applauding those who get it right.

But if you have a chronic bad apple whose behavior doesn't change, don't put up with it. Talk to your fellow managers or your own supervisor about their impact on the team and the work. You're probably not the only one who has experienced it.

If the problem is severe, it may be time for a probation or to let the person go. The best organizations don't put up with sub-par performers, or even brilliant jerks, for long.

Put Awesome Into Action

Name the behavior and be clear about expectations. Find a time to talk one-on-one with your bad apple, and prepare to be a straight shooter. Say things like, "Your attitude this past week has been problematic. I don't expect you or anyone else to be happy about the problem we've come across in this project, but I do expect professionalism and constructive ideas. What's going on and how can I help?" When saying this, your tone should be two-thirds boss and one-third empathetic confidante.

Reward your rock star(s) publicly. You should do this anyway, but it's especially important when dealing with bad apples. Give them a shout-out during a meeting, put them in charge of the most interesting work, or simply stop by to say thanks. If your bad apple catches the drift and starts singing a different tune, definitely make sure to reward them too. Fail to do so, and you'll undo your progress.

Give the bad apple the benefit of the doubt; you might learn something. Ask them questions like, "I heard the concern you brought up. How can I help?" Or, make them own the problem and solution with you: "I've noticed the team is having some issues with the work. What do you think would make a difference?" Giving him or her the chance to influence the solution will often turn bad attitudes around. This one is hard, especially if you're proud like me. If you need to take a walk around the block before or after doing this, I won't judge you.

Know when you've exhausted your options. Talk to your own manager and ask for help. Others are likely aware of the behavior and can let you know what worked for them. Or, it may be time to have a conversation about consequences if expectations aren't met.

Lesson 5:
You Have a Team for a Reason

I still remember my first professional PowerPoint. It was for my parent volunteers; they did talks for groups of low-income parents about how to improve their children's schools.

I worked really hard on that PowerPoint. It was packed with information and the slide background even looked like a chalkboard. Since many of the parents spoke limited English, it was also entirely in Spanish. This predated Google Translate, so I relied on my high school Spanish and the generosity of non-colleague native speakers to translate nuances about California's education policies. Did I mention I worked really hard on it?

My best, rock star volunteer offered to take the most recent speaking engagement I'd lined up. I hadn't seen her in action lately, so I decided to join her.

When it was time to get started, I greeted the parents and introduced my volunteer, willing my Spanish not to fail me. But when my volunteer took over, I didn't need Spanish fluency to realize what was happening. She wasn't following my presentation.

On the ride back, I asked her why she deviated from the slides. It was an honest question; there was no accusation in my tone. And she gave me an honest answer: she tailors her talks based on the group, and some parents respond better to a less-formal style.

Wow. Why didn't I think of that?

The lesson here is simple: you have a team for a reason, and it's so everyone can do work that plays to their strengths. I was great at organizing the program and finding the speaking opportunities. But *she* knew parents. That's why we wanted her as a volunteer, after all.

Even though I was the only paid employee, I still had a team in my volunteers. I should have delegated some or all of the presentation content to them. I could have tasked them with sending me ideas, gotten on the phone for a brainstorm, or asked my rock star volunteer to draft the whole thing. Any of these would have resulted in a better presentation.

* * *

In an effort to learn from this experience, I took it too far in the other direction for much of my early career. I'd assign work with little guidance or direction, not wanting to micromanage or interfere with someone's good ideas.

Then, I'd end up redoing large chunks of their work because it wasn't right.

It took time to find the right balance. I only discovered the key when one of my managers was providing me feedback on something I'd written. She asked, "What can I do in the future so we hit the nail on the head the first time around?"

The key to the balance that was so tough to achieve? Context. Awesome managers don't do (or redo) all the work, nor do they give it all away with vague directions. Instead, they provide context for their teams, like what success looks like, whether some things have to be included, or if anything is totally off-limits.

In Lesson 2, we raised the question *Did I delegate, and did I delegate well?* Here's how you know if you did: by delegating work that others are perfectly capable of doing rather than doing it yourself, being deliberate about who you delegate work to, and making sure you set your people up to succeed by giving clear context.

Remember, as a manager, it's your job to help your team get the work done well—not to do it all yourself.

Put Awesome Into Action

At the beginning of a project, think about the buckets of work and which of your people's strengths are uniquely suited for each bucket. Also, think about the skills or experiences you want each person to gain. Then decide who does what. This takes a lot of practice to get right, even for seasoned managers, because of the foresight involved. Don't be afraid to sit down with your supervisor or another manager for a gut-check on your thinking.

If someone else is capable of doing it, give the work to them. Give the right context and then let it go. Afraid it won't get done right? If you want to be sure you're understood, you can throw in questions like, "Based on what I've shared, how are you going to approach this?" Remember, it looks bad if you hoard work for yourself. Managers aren't supposed to do that. And you'll look like a slacker for doing things that are, comparatively, easy.

Is there a bucket where no one is an obvious fit? Assign it to your rock star. Work side-by-side so s/he learns from you and can do it by themselves next time. It makes you look good when your people grow and become more capable.

Don't micromanage, but be available to help. If you dictate exactly how you want someone to do something, that's a major fail. What if your people find a faster, better or more effective way of doing something? You'll never know because you told them to paint by numbers instead. Give them the context—the goal and any non-negotiable parameters—then stand back and be available to help as needed.

Bring in extra help if you need to. Remember, your job is about removing barriers. If there's a bucket of work that your team is radically under- or overqualified for, look into getting another team member or bring in outside help—specialists, temps, administrative help—if that will help everyone do a better job on their respective assignments.

Don't hold back on feedback. People are thirsty for it. If there's something one of your people can do to improve, find a time when you can discuss it one-on-one—NOT in front of the whole team. Say things like, "The challenge was *[describe the goal]*. Here's where you did a good job. Here's how you could have better addressed the challenge." And, "Knowing what you know now, how would you approach this next time? Is there anything I can do in the future to help?"

Not long after being promoted to the role of vice president at a PR firm, I was given the task of closing a staff retreat with a talk. It was a tough task because it'd been a tough year. Our people were weary.

So I prepared a thoughtful, motivational speech to remind everyone why we were there in the first place and why, despite our challenges, we were lucky because we worked with such remarkable colleagues. I took a deep breath, looked around the table, and launched into it.

And I immediately began crying.

It was not a single, tasteful tear that conveys a professional level of emotion. These were full-blown sobs, the kind where you're gasping like a toddler who fell off a swing. Apparently I, too, was weary.

I managed to talk through the sobs. As soon as it was over, I packed my things and was out the door. The further I walked, the more my horror grew. I frantically texted my manager asking him to be honest and tell me how big of an ass I made of myself. Then I texted my direct report with the same question.

I was suffering from, as researcher and storyteller Brené Brown calls it, a "vulnerability hangover." Every time I replayed the scene in my mind, I died a little. *Who would respect me now?*

* * *

Experts have written about generational differences regarding respect. Baby Boomers, for example, are more likely to respect someone because of their position of authority. Gen Xers and Millennials—the fastest growing group in the workforce—are less likely to respect authority "just because." Instead, they give their respect to leaders who are caring, approachable, and aware.

What this means is if you ever dreamt of saying, "Why? Because I'm the boss, that's why," you can promptly kiss that dream good-bye. Would you respect anyone who said that? Respect is earned by being a person worthy of respect, no matter what your title is.

When it comes to earning respect as a manager, it is better to be loved than feared. And the best way to be loved is to be real.

Too often, managers think they need to be superhuman or better than the people they manage, when in reality nothing could be further from the truth. Yes, as a manager, you need to hold yourself to a higher standard of behavior—to model what you expect of your team. That aside, you want your team to see you as a real human being they can connect with.

My manager and my direct report both texted back right away. They said not to worry and that I did great. I chalked it up to the fact that they could tell I was upset and it was the nice thing to say.

But as it turned out, what I thought was one of my top five most embarrassing moments of all time was actually one of the biggest things I did to boost my credibility as a new VP. People from all levels of the firm thanked me in person and by email for the inspiration. A colleague who wasn't at the retreat told me she heard others singing my praises. I got a round of applause at the next staff meeting.

Not because I cried, but because I was real. I didn't put on a happy face and pretend everything was peachy. I showed that even leaders struggle, but they care, they persevere, and they want things to be better too.

One of my favorite bloggers, Penelope Trunk, once wrote, "Authenticity is magnetic. It makes everyone lean in closer."

It takes bravery to be who you really are, and that will earn you more respect than any title ever will.

Put Awesome Into Action

Ask your team for help, often. No one expects you to be all-knowing. Even the president has advisers. If you're not sure what to do, say so. People will appreciate the honesty and share their ideas. Your job is to make the best decision possible with the information you have.

Think through problems together and be transparent in your decision-making. If a problem arises, talk through options with your team so they understand why it's being handled a certain way. When deciding the best option, explain your logic. For example, "Option A and Option B are both good ideas, but ultimately it's more important for us to be done by our deadline." They don't have to agree, but at least they'll understand your thinking.

Self-censor, just a little. While you want to be authentic and real, it is also your responsibility to keep your team motivated. If you act defeated and say negative things too often, this will rub off on your team. If you need to let off some excess steam, talk to your fellow managers or to your own supervisor. Unless you are the pinnacle of professionalism, you will probably slip up on this one—and you'll feel regret the moment you see your team's reaction to your words. Remember that nobody's perfect; just take a deep breath and move on.

Own up to mistakes. Say things like, "Here's why I thought this was the right decision," or, "I apologize that this mistake means we'll have to *[describe the implications]*." You don't have to beg for forgiveness, but you have to acknowledge what happened. Remember, deep breath.

Be deliberate and consistent about the culture you're creating. Do you want people to take smart risks? Don't punish them if it doesn't pan out. Do you want people to ask for help? Deliver on providing that help. People have to get burned only once before you lose their trust.

It was 4 a.m. My eyes sprung open. I was damp with sweat and felt some kind of intestinal disruption in the works.

No, I didn't have food poisoning or the flu. I was having stress dreams. The kind where everything went wrong and it was all my fault because I'm the manager and I'm supposed to have a handle on everything. So I got up to check my email since we were just over a week away from a big project deadline.

True story. Actually, *stories*, plural, would be more accurate. The downside of managing exciting, challenging work is that the pressure often gets to you.

My friend's husband once told me about his first job at a big bank. His manager was so wound up and stressed that he had a heart attack at work. And even while the EMTs were wheeling him away, he was furiously typing away at emails on his smartphone. As you might imagine, this experience steered my friend's husband into a different industry.

Despite the fact that most of us shake our head upon hearing this story, our culture glorifies this behavior. Wow, he's so dedicated! It's impressive she puts in so many hours! S/he's superhuman!

A more seasoned manager I worked with had a different perspective. She lives by the airplane oxygen-mask rule: make sure your mask is secure before you help others. She prioritizes self-care so she can be a better team member and encourages her people to do the same.

* * *

As a young go-getter, I thought that advice didn't apply to me. And when I crashed, I crashed hard. I was having dinner with my mom, and at one point she stopped me mid-sentence with a surprised look.

"Are...are you okay? I've never seen you like this. You're like a zombie," she said, with perfect motherly concern on her face.

I was like a zombie: my mind was somewhere else, I couldn't form coherent sentences, my skin was pale. But I didn't have time to take a vacation. The deadline was looming.

Trust me, you don't want this to be you. Not only will you be miserable, but the smart higher-ups are looking at all the managers and noticing the ones who get great results *without* driving themselves and their teams into a pit of despair and burnout. That's who they're going to promote—not the stress-monger who has to work twice as hard to get the same results.

This isn't to say that you shouldn't put in extra effort and hours when the stakes are high. But that shouldn't be your, or your team's, general M.O.

My zombie-like state hadn't improved, even after the weekend. When I got out of the shower, I wasn't sure I'd even remembered to wash my hair. I wasn't going to be of any use to anyone. So I did the unthinkable: with only a few days leading up to our deadline, I called in sick. I told my team that I'd be unavailable that day and turned my cell phone and computer off.

It doesn't sound that dramatic, does it? That's the whole point. I was so wrapped up in this deadline that I'd lost all perspective. All I could see was the pressure and the things that were going wrong, instead of the opportunities and the things that were going right.

When I went into work the next day, I was pleasantly surprised to find that the world had not ended. I could drop off the radar for 24 hours and the work would still be there waiting for me. My team could figure out a way to overcome minor roadblocks on their own. With a distinctly non-zombie-like energy, I started my day.

In the end, we still met the big deadline. But it would have been a whole lot less painful if I'd secured my mask first. It also showed in the quality of my team's work: we did good, but we could have done great.

People with unhealthy amounts of stress make careless mistakes, overlook opportunities for innovation, and lose their longing for the sea. Your team is more likely to work hard for you if you're modeling healthy behavior and making their lives better, not worse.

So be an awesome manager by taking care of yourself, and taking care of your team. It'll pay off in more ways than one.

Put Awesome Into Action

Know when you're approaching your breaking point. If you start having stress dreams or are staring blankly at your bowl of oatmeal for 30 minutes, take a personal or sick day—or even two. That's what they're there for. Tell your team they can call you if it's an emergency, but otherwise you'll be unavailable until the next day. Don't look at your email. Go for a run, bake a cake, do some yoga, have a beer with lunch, or go on a day trip. The work will be there tomorrow; take care of you today.

Look out for others who are struggling. If someone else on your team is in a bad place, ask them what they have to get done that day, find a way to postpone it or take it on yourself, and make them take a personal day. They'll come back re-energized and may be able to help take something off another team member's plate so everyone can practice self-care.

Create opportunities for frequent check-ins. You'll feel more peace of mind if you have your finger on the pulse of what's going on. During particularly intense periods, create a 10-minute "standing meeting" first thing in the morning where everyone stands around a table and agrees on priorities for the day. Or, use a program like iDoneThis to get no-frills status updates at the end of every day so you're in the know. Do this as a team, not one-on-one, as it builds momentum for everyone to see what they're a part of and progress being made.

Listen to your stress. Sometimes it's our gut's way of saying we need to pay attention to something. If something is stressing you out, take five minutes to ask yourself why. Then, put that item in your Zorro Circle.

I hope you enjoyed this guide and have already started using these ideas at work. If you have, then you're probably starting to get acquainted with that "awesome manager" feeling.

It's a combination of satisfaction, excitement, and pride. You feel it when one of your people does something amazing because you removed a barrier for them. Or when they surprised you with incredible work you didn't even know they were capable of. Or when they stopped by your office and said, "Thank you."

Enjoy that feeling. It's one of the best things about being a manager.

Rather than asking you for your thanks, I'd ask you to, instead, pay it forward and share this wisdom with other new managers you know.

You can share these lessons and recommended reads with other managers at your job, gift this guide to a friend or colleague who was recently promoted, or leave a brief review on Amazon to help spread the word.

If you'd like to give me any feedback personally or ask any questions, I would love to hear from you. You can email me at murray.tamara.a@gmail.com or follow and message me at @tamaramurray on Twitter.

Lastly, the most important thing you can do to pay it forward is to just be an awesome manager in every job you have. The world could use more awesome managers. Think of what we can accomplish!

Resources and Recommended Reading

Save time! Visit HelloImTamara.com/Resources for links to each of these reads.

On motivation and delegation:

- Crucial Tips On Delegating The Right Way, So Everyone Wins (Fast Company)
- Getting Colleagues to Carry Their Weight (LinkedIn)
- The Power of the Done List (iDoneThis)
- How to Run Wildly Unproductive Meetings and Waste Everyone's Time (Brazen Careerist)

On work-life balance:

- You Aren't Indestructible or Indispensable — And That's Good (LinkedIn)
- Please Stop Complaining About How Busy You Are (Harvard Business Review)
- Defry Your Burnt Brain: 4 Quick Ways to Unplug in the Afternoon (Fast Company)
- How to Defeat Burnout and Stay Motivated (Zenhabits)

On leadership:

- Qualities Of A Leader: How To Go from "Good Manager" To "Great Leader" (Barking Up The Wrong Tree)
- Most Productive People: Wendy Clark (Fast Company)
- The new authenticity: More nuanced than simple transparency (Penelope Trunk)

- How to Escape from Bad Decisions (LinkedIn)
- Brené Brown: The power of vulnerability (TED)
- Leadership Challenge: How Lovable Are You? (Inc)
- Myths About Millennials (About.com)

More blogs and publications to follow:

- 99U
- Barking Up The Wrong Tree
- Fast Company, especially the sections Leadership Now and 30-Second MBA
- Harvard Business Review
- Inc. Magazine
- Penelope Trunk

Tamara Murray learned she had a knack for management and leadership when people kept asking her to do it, despite her lack of formal management training. At 16, as the youngest employee, she was promoted to assistant manager at a retail store. At 20, she managed cadres of parent and student volunteers at two nonprofits. At 22, she had a steady stream of interns under her purview. And at 26, a PR firm put her on its senior team, responsible for managing multiple account teams and clients. In every role, she managed people the same age or older, often with more experience and credentials.

She found her footing through a combination of trial and error, reading a lot of *Fast Company*, and having the occasional breakdown in a colleague's office. Eventually, people started using phrases like "one-of-a-kind leader," "brings out the best in everyone," and "trusted to deliver results," to describe her management style. She's a firm believer that you don't need an MBA (and massive student loans) to be an awesome manager.

Originally from San Francisco, she set off to travel Latin America in October 2013 with her husband, Chris, and their dog, Holly, to gain perspective, research their next projects, and learn to make killer refried beans. Follow her for work/life reads and travel advice on Twitter at @tamaramurray or learn more about her other projects: www.HelloImTamara.com.